The Studebaker Brothers: The Lives and Legacy of the Family Behind the Famous Automobile Company

By Charles River Editors

The five Studebaker brothers

Introduction

A 1912 Studebaker bus

"The automobile has come to stay. But when a man has no business, it is a rather expensive luxury, and I would advise no man, be he farmer or merchant, to buy one until he has sufficient income to keep it up. A horse and buggy will afford a great deal of enjoyment…" – John M. Studebaker

For a couple of generations of Americans, along with Ford, Chrysler, and General Motors, there was Studebaker, and though it is no longer in existence, the Studebaker Automobile Company is still part of the popular culture. When a 1950s family is depicted on television today, the likelihood is that the family car is a Studebaker. The symbolic power of the Studebaker name was recently exemplified when South Bend, Indiana Mayor Pete Buttigieg announced his candidacy for the Democratic Party's presidential nomination. Kris Maher, writing in *The Wall Street Journal*, noted "For decades, the biggest symbol of this Midwestern city's decline was the vacant Studebaker plant at one end of the city with its broken windows. Kevin Smith, a business owner in South Bend who bought the property to renovate it, said the empty relic was holding the city back. 'It looms over the town,' he said. 'Everyone had the feeling that we could no longer compete. These days, some 40 organizations, including tech companies and a school that teaches coding to children, rent space on the 1.2 million-square-foot campus, including one building with an open floor plan and interior glass walls. Now called the Renaissance District, it is a symbol of the rebound in the state's fourth-largest city.'"

Today, people have likely heard of the name Studebaker without realizing that before Detroit was dominated by the Big Three automakers, there was a fourth major automobile company. The story of the Studebaker company and the Studebaker family exemplifies both the American dream and the difficulty in sustaining that dream.

The Studebaker Brothers: The Lives and Legacy of the Family Behind the Famous Automobile Company chronicles how the family built up a manufacturing empire and made some of America's most famous cars. Along with pictures of important people, places, and events, you will learn about the Studebaker brothers like never before.

South Bend

"To have integrity the individual cannot merely be a weathervane turning briskly with every doctrinal wind that blows. He must possess key loyalties and key convictions which can serve as a basis of judgment and a standard of action." – John Studebaker

The Studebaker story begins in Germany. The family originated in the Ruhr Valley in the town of Solingen, southwest of Dusseldorf, and during the late 17th century the region had been subjected to war, heavy taxation, and religious strife. Thus, Peder and Clemens Studebecker decided to emigrate, but in order to leave, the local guild required them to move to another city and work for five years. The brothers moved to Hagen, to the northeast of Solingen, where Peter met and married Anna Aschauer in 1725 and Clement was married to Anna Melchers in 1729. In 1736, Peter, Clemens, and their wives, along with a cousin, emigrated to Philadelphia in 1736. They arrived at the port of Philadelphia on September 1 of that year on the ship *Harle*, sailing from Rotterdam.

By 1798, according to the tax records of York County, Pennsylvania, Peter Studebaker, Sr. and Peter Studebaker, Jr. were employed as wagon makers, laying the foundation for the Studebaker family fortune.

John Studebaker was born on February 8, 1799 in Adams County, Pennsylvania, and in 1820 he married Rebecca Mohler in Ephrata, Pennsylvania. He built a house and workshop near present-day Gettysburg in 1830, where he worked as a blacksmith and wagon maker, but his business struggled because the country was going through a prolonged economic slump in the aftermath of the Panic of 1819. Within five years, he was deeply in debt and sold his holdings in Pennsylvania.

In 1835, John built a covered wagon and moved his family to Ashland, Ohio. By this time, his family included his wife Rebeca, his son Henry (born in 1826), his son Clement (born in 1831), and his son John Mohler (born in 1833). A fourth son, Peter, was born in 1836 after they had relocated to Ohio, and Peter was followed eight years later by Jacob Franklin. In addition, the family included five daughters.

John Studebaker

Clement Studebaker

Peter Studebaker

In Ashland, John bought property and reestablished himself as a blacksmith and wagon builder. Once again, however, he and his family lived frugally and struggled for several years, and he was ultimately forced to mortgage his property to pay his creditors. Continuing to search for a better life, John left Henry in charge of his business and went west to Indiana, where he visited a town later known as South Bend. Seeing it as an ideal place to get a new start, he returned to Ashland to prepare his family for another move. Clement went ahead and found work in South Bend at the Eliakim Briggs Threshing Machine Works, and later he got a job teaching. In late 1851, John and the remainder of the family left Ohio for South Bend.

John Mohler Studebaker described the family's first home in South Bend: "There were nine of us living then in an old log cabin which contained one room beside the kitchen. On either side of the great fire place were the beds for the younger children, with trundle beds beneath which we pulled out at night for the babies. As each grew older he slept in the left underneath the roof, which was reached by a ladder. There was always a basket of apples and a big earthen pitcher of cider. There were no chairs so we used rough benches. The cups were bright colored gourds grown in our garden. The plates were of pewter. In the winter when the cider was very cold, my father kept a soldering iron, which he would heat over the logs and plunge into the pitcher until the cider was warm. Clothes were a simple matter as to style. My mother spun the yarn, wove the cloth and sewed the garments for herself and us children. Until I was 10 years old I wore dresses because you see they were so much easier to make than pants."

In South Bend, the brothers began to follow their father's advice and get an independent start in life. In 1852, Henry and Clement opened their own business, H & C Studebaker, as a blacksmith and wagonbuilding shop. They began with capital of $68 and two forges.

John Mohler, then 19, decided to try his hand in the recently discovered gold fields of California, so he traveled to Hangtown (now Placerville) in 1853. As he would learn firsthand, while the Gold Rush will always conjure images of miners trying to find gold, most of the wealth was not in the hands of the miners in the fields but in the hands of the people trying to cater to the miners and sell them goods. Years later, he would recount his experiences in California: "We were more than five months on the road, and landed right here on this square in August, 1853, and I had but fifty cents in my pocket. Although that was my only earthly possession, my spirit was not daunted, for we were all led to believe that all we had to do was to go out on the morrow and dig all the gold that the heart could desire. Of course, a big crowd gathered around us, and while we were trying to get them to talk about the gold mines, they insisted on asking questions about what had happened in the States since they had heard from their friends. While the hubbub was going on, a man came up and asked if there was a wagon-maker in the crowd of new arrivals. They pointed me out, and he asked, 'Are you a wagon- maker?' 'Yes sir,' I answered, as big as life, with my fifty-cent piece in my pocket. He offered me a job in his shop, and I replied, 'I came to California to mine for gold.' After he had gone, a man stepped up very politely and said, 'Will you let me give you a little advice, young man ? ' and upon my replying in the affirmative, continued, 'Take that job and take it quick'. His manner impressed me. He said that there would be plenty of time to dig gold, it wasn't always a sure thing, and that the job just offered me was a mighty fine chance for a stranger. I was impressed, and decided to go to work for the wagon-maker. He wanted me to make wheelbarrows for the miners, and arranged to pay me ten dollars each for my work. The tools were poor, and material only pitch pine lumber. I stuck to the job, made many wheelbarrows, and put my money in the bank. I soon found that hundreds and thousands of the pioneers who tried the mines never made a cent, but those who stuck to steady jobs at good wages and saved their money were doing well. We worked many a night all night, frequently making miners' picks and repairing stage coaches, which came in late, and had to get out at six o'clock in the morning."

In South Bend, Henry and Clement were suffering some difficult times and having a hard time financing the business. As Albert Russel Erskine described it, they faced problems not unfamiliar to small businesses in rural communities in 1850s America: "They had few tools, bought their material as needed from a local hardware store, and usually traded their wagons to farmers for livestock or crops, or took notes in payment. Money was scarce and seldom obtained for sales." They were receiving wagon orders, but in their current situation they could only turn out a dozen wagons a year.

Erskine

A Change in Fortunes

In 1857, the United States Army had contracted with the Mishawaka Wagon Works near South Bend to manufacture several hundred wagons, and upon realizing they could not fulfill the contract on their own, Mishawaka approached the Studebaker brothers for assistance. Henry and Clement agreed to deliver 100 wagons in six months, but to do so, they would have to hire and train help and obtain the necessary lumber. They looked to the woods around South Bend, and in order to cure the wood properly for the wagons, they built drying kilns. Everything else they needed was either fabricated, contrived, or farmed out.

The wagons were delivered in 90 days, yet the firm made little profit. Henry and Clement had created the infrastructure to turn out wagons in large numbers, but they lacked the capital, so the brothers turned to their brother John M. for assistance. From his enterprises in Placerville, John M. had saved about $8,000.00 in gold, and Henry and Clement eventually managed to persuade John M. to return to South Bend and join the business. In April 1858, John sold his business in Placerville and took passage on a sailing ship for New York via the Isthmus of Panama. When he arrived in South Bend, John M. bought out Henry's share in the business. It appears that Henry had become concerned about building equipment for the Amy, in part because he was a Dunkard Brethren, a variety of conservative German Baptists who preached pacifism and non-violence. As Stephen Longstreet, in the official history of the Studebaker company, succinctly put it,

"Henry was tired of the business. He wanted to farm. The risks of expanding were not for him"

John M.'s investment stabilized the firm's financial situation and laid the foundation for future expansion. They continued to manufacture wagons for westward migration as well as for farming and general transportation.

Soon after John M. returned to South Bend, he was introduced to Mary Jane Stull, a friend of his sister Sally. Mary Jane would later record their first meeting: "When they arrived and we were introduced, I can not tell you how disappointed I was...The young man about whom I had begun to think somewhat was just off from a Panama boat, having gone around the Horn on a sailing vessel to get home. His face was the color of a well-born Indian, and after being sea sick during the entire trip, his big nose and bony face had anything but an attractive appearance."

After this first brief meeting, John M. returned a week later, and to Mary Jane he seemed to be a different man: "When he came in he took me off my high stilts as he was beautifully dressed in a brand-new light trousers, silk brocaded waistcoat and a shining new frock coat with a light felt hat to match his trousers. He surely looked like a new man to me. I was very chatty and coy and I am sure I must have made a favorable impression as he asked me to go riding with him the next Sunday. My husband when young was much given to wearing jewelry made from California gold nuggets which he plentifully displayed on his shirt front, sleeve buttons and watch chain, and two of his fingers were ornamented with gold bands. At one time he came out to see me in his regalia, which I thought was very fine, but the practical eyes of my father saw deeper than a love-sick maid and he disapproved of so much display. A gentleman who was at our house and knew Mr. Studebaker heard these criticisms and told him that my father had said that he had too much gold hanging about him for a right-minded, sensible young man. This ended all jewelry forever afterwards when he came to see me. By this time things were moving along so rapidly in our love affairs that all of my other sweethearts had disappeared like mist in sunshine, leaving the coast clear to the California lover, who about this time went to Philadelphia to see some relatives and while there had actually the audacity to propose to me by letter. We were married on a cold winter day, the second of January 1860, in my father's house."

After the wedding, Mary Jane described their honeymoon, particularly the journey they had reaching their destination: "We were whirled to the railroad station through the blinding ice and cold, way down below zero. Our horses were completely covered with ice after their two mile run from my home, and when we got into the car we found it freezing cold and every one growling. We were going on to Chicago, but rather than endure such discomforts we left the car at LaPorte, remained there all night and took an early train back, passing through home and going to visit a brother of my husband who lived in Goshen. Mr. Peter Studebaker and his charming young wife were somewhat surprised when we walked in upon them unexpectedly, but our explanations soon cleared things up and we remained there a week, no one knowing where we were."

Mary Jane

As the firm's operations expanded, a fourth brother entered the business. Peter E. Studebaker was the fourth oldest of the brothers, and he was 15 when the family moved to South Bend. He soon took a position as a store clerk for $15 a month, and after saving what he could from his salary, Peter invested $100 in stock and became an itinerant peddler. He remained a peddler until he was induced to settle down by meeting and marrying Dora Handley. They settled in Goshen, Indiana, and Peter became partners with Philip Welch, the husband of his sister Sally, in a general store. When Henry and Clement asked him to join them in the business, Peter agreed and expanded his store to include the sale of wagons.

As sales increased, Clement and John M. expanded the factory, to the extent that by 1860, they employed 14 men in the making of wagons. They also expanded into carriages, designing and manufacturing a phaeton beginning in 1857.

A phaeton design from 1850

With the beginning of the Civil War, the Studebaker company entered a period of expansion. While their religious scruples did not allow them to serve in the Army, Clement and John M. did not share Henry's objections when it came to accepting government contracts to supply wagons to the Army. Beginning in 1862, the federal government placed orders for wagons, gun cassons, and ambulances, and the wagons were of such good quality that Confederate troops often captured them for their own use after battles. By 1867, the Studebaker brothers had manufactured over 6,000 vehicles for the Army, and they had provided carriages that would be used by several presidents, including Abraham Lincoln, Ulysses S. Grant, and Rutherford B. Hayes. Meanwhile, the factory had grown to cover four acres of land in South Bend and employed 140 mechanics.

To draw attention to their expansion, the brothers published the following advertisement in May 1867: "The great failure at South Bend, Indiana of Studebaker Bros. heretofore to supply the people of Northern Indian and Southern Michigan with their superior Carriages, Buggies, and Farm Wagons has induced them to take this method of informing the public that they have greatly increased their facilities for manufacturing by introducing new machinery of the latest invention, enlarging their factory and securing the services of the most skillful and experienced mechanics in the country. They are thus enabled to turn out the most perfect work and in such quantities as to be able to supply all desirous of purchasing. They especially call the attention of Farmers to their present style of Farm Wagons. Having secured the services of Mr. H. W. Ingersoll to superintend our woodwork department and Mr. P. F. Ingersoll as master blacksmith, who are well known to be two of the most accomplished mechanics in the west we feel confident in claiming that our heavy work does and shall stand unrivalled in this country for strength durability and finish. Our timber is of the best quality and thoroughly seasoned undercover and we employ only the best mechanics in all departments of our business. Farmers! If you wish to buy double wagons, carriages or buggies, or anything else in our line, do not fail to come to South Bend and examine our work before purchasing and we pledge ourselves to satisfy you that we do not exaggerate and that our prices are such as will meet the exigencies of short crops or any other misfortune."

On January 1, 1868, the net assets of H & C Studebaker were $223,269.06, with sales of almost $350,000 annually. Not surprisingly, the business had outgrown Henry and Clement's original business structure, so on March 26, 1868, Studebaker Brothers Manufacturing Company was incorporated in the State of Indiana. The initial capitalization was $75,000, with $25,000 divided to each of the brothers. Clement was named President, John M. was named Treasurer, and Peter was named Secretary. Each brother received salaries of $2,000 per year, and they divided the responsibilities for overseeing the company. Clement attended to administrative matters, John M. oversaw the construction of wagons and carriages, and Peter used his sales skills to create markets outside of Indiana.

The expansion of the Studebaker Brothers Manufacturing Company came at a cost to John M. in particular, as the hours of hard work took their toll on him. In 1869 he began coughing up blood. Mary Jane later recalled that the doctors diagnosed him as being overworked, and they prescribed a trip to Europe: "When my husband became sufficiently strong we arranged our affairs, made our wills and were baptized in the St. Joseph River by Mr. Forsyth, the Presbyterian preacher. With our consciences at ease and our worldly possessions taken care of, we left our two little girls in the care of my brother and sister, who lived on a large farm on Sumption Prairie. England and Switzerland and spending one winter in Italy. The sunshine and change in the old world did not improve my husband's health as we had expected, and after remaining there more than a year we returned home to our children and friends."

Unfortunately, John M.'s health began to worsen, resulting in another trip. Mary Jane wrote, "The winter after our return from Europe began to tell upon my husband's health so that he was obliged to seek a warmer climate. I was not able to go with him, so he took his man and went to Georgia, hoping that the sunshine and mild breezes might give him back his health and strength. While he was there he was told of a wonderful spring in Tennessee, the waters of which had brought back health to many weary ill people. Catching at every promise which looked even favorable he at once let and found in the mountains of eastern Tennessee the water of life for his worn tired body. When I met him at the station [that Christmas] I never would have known him if it had not been for the beaming eyes and the pleasant smile. He really was not the same man who had left us so short a time ago. All the sick, work look had gone from his face. His checks had lost their paleness and were filled with good new flesh, tinted with fresh blood which he had gained from these healing waters. He continued to gain flesh and strength all through the rest of the winter and early spring he went back, taking me and the children with him. For a number of years he made a pilgrimage to old Tate Spring, always gaining new health and strength until at last he entirely regained his health and went back to business a new man."

St. Joseph, Missouri served as the staging point for wagon trains heading west, and each spring, masses of new settlers departed from the town. When doing so, they needed wagons to make the long trek across the open prairie, vehicles durable enough to transport their families and their goods to their new homesteads. With that in mind, the brothers decided to have Peter relocate to St. Joseph to set up a sales outlet there, and around 1870, Peter and his brother-in-law set up the first Studebaker showroom outside of Indiana. The *Lawrence Daily Journal* wrote of the Studebaker effort, "It is not generally known, but it is nevertheless a fact, that Studebaker Bros., the great carriage and wagon manufacturers, have the largest repository at ST. Joseph, Mo., west of New York. Their building is 60x40, two stories high, and it is filled with carriages, buffies, express and skeleton wagons, of all styles and prices. Their work is too well known to need to comment, and hence we would just say to any one needing anything in the above line, that they can find a better stock, and at lower prices than they can be bought at either in St. Louis or Chicago. A good stock of carriages is what the West has long needed, and we doubt not the public will profit by this enterprise of the Studebaker brothers."

In a few years, Peter would establish Studebaker showrooms in Salt Lake, San Francisco, Kansas City, Portland, Dallas, Minneapolis, Chicago, New York and Denver. In 1870, total sales were in excess of $500,000.

As a result, the company entered the 1870s in very good shape. By 1872, the Studebaker factory consisted of two buildings. The main building was a block long and four stories tall, while the second building, which stood behind it, was a three-story building spouting 30 smokestacks. There was a detailed description of the factory published in the South Bend City Directory that year. Among other things, it said, "The traveler on the Lake Shore & Michigan Southern Railway...observes an immense pile of buildings of brick and stone, with Mansard roof and various architectural adornments. The general contour is elegant, impressive and immense. The walls are massive and the proportions according to the best rules of art, giving the beholder an impression of solidity and adaptation to substantial uses. The style is modern, ornate, beautiful, yet with special reference to the great business purposes to which it is dedicated. Every part is strong and substantial. The general appearance of the building leads many to suppose it to be a college or some other institution of learning, and so it is, for here is taught the art of wagon making, and under the tuition of learned industrial professors, young men are prepared for posts of usefulness and honor. The width of this immense building is 62 feet, in length it is 868 feet. The structure is partly three and partly six stories. The outside linear measurement is about a half mile. Its floorage is over five acres, while the other buildings for storage, drying, &c. Cover about two and a quarter acres!"

The Directory description also described the full extent of the Studebaker property: "The ground actually occupied for wagon factory, carriage shops, offices, repositories, dry-houses, lumber sheds, &c., comprise thirteen and three-eights acres. Of this land ten and one-forth acres are in one compact body, lying directly south of and adjoining the depot grounds of the Lake Shore & Michigan Southern Railway. A substantial brick fence or wall will inclose the premises...In the northeast corner, elegant offices, with fire-proof vaults, and all possible conveniences are provided. The shipping rooms open upon the track of the L. S. & M. S. Railway, and are very commodious and convenient. But this is not all. On Jefferson and Michigan streets are the large coach and carriage factory of this company, occupying three-fourths of an acre. The building is 320 by 44 feet. The outside linear measurement is 728 feet. The north elevation is 100 by 44 feet, four stories above basement. The south elevation 122 by 50 feet two stories. All are brick. The total floorage is one and a quarter acres. Here are found blacksmith shops, with 35 forges, wood shops, painting, varnishing and trimming rooms, storage rooms, repository, &c. The machinery is driven by a forty-horse power engine."

The Directory was particularly impressed with the production and output of the Studebaker plant: "The easy capacity of the works is over 15,000 wagons per annum, and carriages and other fine work without limit giving employment to 500 men in the various departments. Three and a half million pounds of iron and five million feet of timber are used annually. We may further add as an item calculated to impress the mind with the magnitude of these works that over three million of brick and two and a half million feet of lumber have been used in their construction."

A fire in June 1872 caused $70,000 worth of damage to the main building, but because of the business' sound financial footing, the losses to the company were kept to a minimum. Jan Young provided an extensive description of the fire: "The 1872 fire started shortly before 6 o'clock in the afternoon on Monday, June 17, 1872 in the plant's woodworking shop at the corner of Lafayette and South streets in South Bend. The shop, of course, generated large quantities of shavings and sawdust and a blower was used to carry the waste to another room for storage pending disposal. One of the journals of the blower overheated, firing the dust, but the blower continued to run long enough to carry the fire into the storage area, which went up in flames in a matter of seconds. The workmen saved themselves only by immediate flight. Fire alarms were sounded and the response was immediate. The Third Ward engine, being the closest, arrived first and tried to pull water out of the well at the corner of Lafayette and South streets, but to no avail because the well…was dry. For some time, only one engine was able to actually apply water to the fire by taking it from nearby Lake Shore and Michigan Southern Railroad's water tank."

A crowd of several thousand gathered to watch the fire, and many helped fight it since it was in danger of spreading to the surrounding area. Not surprisingly, the fire had a lot of potential kindling rather near it, as Young noted: "Across Lafayette street from the Studebaker plant was a lumber yard. Lines of men passed buckets from hand to hand and every available pump was kept running to bring water from the few places where it could be found. The lumber yard was mostly saved, but a house next to it was lost, as was one belonging to John Myers, next to the Studebaker plant. A barn behind the Myers house and another barn nearby went up in flames. Three more barns east of the plant were taken. The roof of the 3rd Ward school caught fire from the sparks raining down on it and the building was nearly lost."

As bad as the fire was, it could have been a lost worse for Studebaker since the building that burned had been bought in 1867. Young pointed out, "In 1871...the Studebakers had bought the first portion of what was to become the Studebaker automobile plant on the south side of the tracks and had erected buildings there and began production. The company's valuable inventory of dried and drying lumber was also stored at the new plant and was not touched by the fire. And the carriage and blacksmith shops...were unaffected. The brothers, therefore, lost an important facility, but didn't lose everything."

More problematic for the long-term viability of the company was the Panic of 1873, the biggest economic downturn in the nation's history. It was triggered by the collapse of the large banking house Jay Cooke & Co., which had heavily financed railroads after the Civil War before a collapse in investment after the discovery of the Credit Mobilier fraud resulted in the firm losing capital at an alarming rate. They announced the suspension of withdrawals on September 18, 1873, stating, "The immediate cause of suspension of Jay Cooke & Co. was the large drawing upon them by the Philadelphia house and their own depositors during the last fortnight. Both houses had suffered a large draw upon their deposits in consequence of the uneasy feeling which has recently prevailed, and which has affected, more or less, all houses closely identified with new railroad enterprises."

The *New York Times* on September 19, 1873 described the panic on Wall Street: "The first intimation which came into the Stock Exchange of any change in the programme was contained in a brief notice, which said authoritatively that Jay Cooke & Co. had suspended payment. To say that the street became excited would only give a feeble view of the expressions of feeling. The brokers stood perfectly thunderstruck for a moment, and then there was a general run to notify the different houses in Wall street of the failure...The members of the firms who were surprised by this announcement had no time to deliberate. The bear clique was already selling the market down in the Exchange, and prices were declining frightfully...Some of the men who were ruined swore, some of them wept, some went out of the street without saying a word; others talked of the trouble in a jovial way and went about trying to borrow money from friends."

Thomas Klitgaard and James Narron explained the effects: "The panic led to bank runs and bank failures, followed by commercial bankruptcies and unemployment so severe that the downturn was called the Great Depression at the time. It lasted so long, more than five years, that it is now known as the Long Depression." As with most industrial firms, the STudebaker Brothers suffered from the economic downturn, but not initially; they ended 1873 with a record of $820,000 in sales. To prepare for a prolonged downturn, they tightened their belts where possible, going from producing a wagon every 10 minutes to a wagon every 20 minutes. They did not pay a dividend to shareholders in 1874, but the company survived, benefitting from a reduced price for ram materials for use in the manufacture of wagons.

More troubling than the financial panic was another fire at the plant on August 24, 1874, this one much larger than the 1872 conflagration. Jan Young also described this fire: "The fire began in the paint shop, probably caused by spontaneous combustion. It was discovered at 4:30 AM by two passengers who were waiting at the Lake Shore & Michigan Southern station for the early morning train to Chicago. The alarm was turned in immediately. This time, fire service was more effective than in 1872, but the city's steam pumper failed after only a few hours' work and the fire fighters were limited to the pressure available from the newly installed standpipe. James Mills, Studebaker's chief bookkeeper, arrived on the 4:50 AM train and immediately dashed into the general office and removed at least some of the company's books and papers from the vault in the office building. Railroad cars parked at the plant were quickly removed by the railroad and there was concern at one point that the railroad depot might take fire. But, with eight hoses playing on the flames, the fire was successfully brought under control in about two hours and was completely out by sundown. Surprisingly, only two injuries were listed; J. M. Studebaker burned himself slightly while trying to close a hot door, and a fireman was hit by rubble when a wall collapsed. The early hour of the fire and the fact that the building was empty at the time doubtlessly prevented many other injuries."

The fire was devastating to the company, and Young listed the damage: "The 1874 fire destroyed most of the new plant that had been built south of the railroad tracks only two years earlier. The paint department, the general offices, the shipping department, the iron house and the blacksmith department were completely lost. Also lost were 2,100 finished wagons stored in the building awaiting shipment. The boiler and engine rooms, the carpentry department, a number of outlying buildings, and Studebaker's supply of green and drying lumber were all saved, as was the remaining portion of the old plant on the north side of the track."

The Studebaker Bros.' Wagon Works, with View of the Ruins, the Unburned Buildings, Lumber Sheds, Etc.

A contemporary sketch of the property after the fire

Undeterred, the Studebaker brothers rebuilt. The new factory was reconstructed almost totally in four months included extensive fire protection equipment and was the world's largest carriage and wagon works, covering 20 acres and capable of turning out a wagon every ten minutes. So remarkable was the speed of reconstruction that the Studebaker brothers built and shipped over 2,500 vehicles. In 1875, less than a year removed from the fire and in the midst of the economic downturn, Studebaker Brothers' sales topped $1,000,000.

The youngest Studebaker brother, Jacob, joined the business in 1875 and was put in charge of the carriage works. In *History of St. Joseph County*, Timothy Howard outlined his role in the business: "Practical ability of the highest order, combined with the warm trains f humanity and an invariable consideration for the rights and feelings of others, are qualities which mark the Studebakers as a family, and the late Jacob F. Studebaker inherited these family traits in their full strength...The Studebaker Brothers Manufacturing Company is one of the distinctively great industries of the world, and none of its departments are more favorably known that that devoted to the output of carriages, with which Jacob F. was so long identified as manager. His brothers Clem, J. M. and Peter E. were proud to give him full credit for his admirable business and personal qualities. Methodically and surely he advanced from post to post until as manager of the carriage department he was one of the most important personal forces connected with the great industry. Under the stimulus of his practical knowledge and keen foresight the branch of the business under his direct supervision reached mammoth proportions. He was energetic and straight-forward, at the same time kind and considerate to those in his employ. The nature of Mr. Studebaker's specialty in the business of the company necessarily brought him in contact with the owners and lovers of horses, and he himself became one of the most enthusiastic horsemen in the country. He possessed some of the stars of the turf, but his particular admiration was the Percheron, and he organized the great Percheron Horse Company of Colorado, which has been the means of importing some of the finest specimens of that breed ever brought to the United States."

Jacob Studebaker

1876 marked the 100th anniversary of the nation's founding, and the Centennial International Exhibition was held in Philadelphia, Pennsylvania from May-November of that year. Featured in its large exhibition halls were various inventions and examples of the fruits of American manufacturers, including several Studebaker products. Thomas Kinney, in his history of the manufacture of horse drawn vehicles in America, noted, "When the nation's manufacturers displayed their goods at Philadelphia's 1876 Centennial Exposition, the Studebaker Brothers Manufacturing Company was present, and not just in the farm wagon building. Over in the Main Annex, a Studebaker top buggy stood in a long row of carriages by such luminaries as Rufus Stivers, the Brewstes, and William D. Rogers, and the South Bend firm came away with awards." The awards were a gold medal and the Highest Award of Merit.

A Changing of the Guard

By the late 1870s, Studebaker customers could choose a wide variety of wheeled horse-drawn vehicles, including sulkies, broughams, clarences, phaetons, runabouts, victorias, and tandems, and a customer could purchase a four-in-hand for $20,000 that would carry up to a dozen passengers.

In 1884, Jacob opened a carriage sales and service operation in Chicago. The Studebaker Building was designed by S. S. Benman and built between 1885 and 1887 on Michigan Avenue, sporting two 12-foot-tall granite columns at the entrance. The *Chicago Tribune* wrote in 1886, "The great Studebaker Building on Michigan avenue, below Van Buren street, is nearing completion. It will be recognized as one of the chief landmarks of the city, worthy at once of Chicago and of the great manufacturing house of which it will be representative. The error of a lady the other day in mistaking the building for the American Institute of Art, situated just to the north, was quite natural, for certainly those immense shafts of polished granite at the entrance to the Studebaker Building are the most artistic things on all Michigan avenue. The Chicago Carriage Repository of this manufacturing company is one of the finest houses of the kind in the city. The general offices and factories are located at South Bend, Ind. In a humble blacksmith shop in that· town, in 1850, the father of the Studebaker Brothers pursued his toilsome vocation, earning his daily bread and bringing up his boys to a knowledge of the anvil and the forge. Thirty-four years have wrought a great change. The carriage and wagon works of the brothers and the buildings immediately adjacent, cover over thirty acres of land (including lumber-yards, etc., eighty acres); and their wagons and carriages have now, in the broad field of competition, a world-wide renown and have achieved great triumphs wherever they have entered the lists of the World's industries. At hundreds of local and State expositions many verdicts have been adjudged in their favor. At the National Fair at Chicago, in 1867, they were awarded the first prize for excellence. At the United States Exposition in 1876, they led all the Centennial awards. At the World's Great Fair, at Paris, in 1878, they were awarded the silver medal, and the same by the Mexican Republic in 1879. Thirty-five years ago they were humble blacksmiths; to-day, beyond doubt, they are the largest carriage and wagon manufacturers in the world. They have five repositories in the United States, the one in Chicago being made a leading feature. The members of the company are all residents of South Rend, Ind. Their repository was established here in 1874. Wilbur F. Studebaker, son of P. E. Studebaker, treasurer of the company, is the resident manager, and has been one of Chicago's citizens for about six years. The building now in course of erection on Michigan Avenue, is one of the finest buildings on the American continent, and is a tribute as well to the enterprise of the firm as to our city."

In 1895, less than eight years after its completion, the Studebaker Company announced a remodeling of the building. At that time, the *Chicago Tribune* reported, "The Studebaker Building (remodeling), at Nos. 378 to 388 Wabash avenue, is nearly completed. Its cost is $250,O00. In size it is 120×150 feet. The Studebaker Bros. Manufacturing company, for whom the building is built, will occupy the main floor, basement, and second floor, and the balance of the ten stories will be divided to suit tenants. The building contains some novel features in the way of plate glass fronts, making it one of the lightest buildings for salerooms in Chicago. The front and rear of the building contain 95 per cent, making it the lightest building in the city. In addition to this feature there is a light court in the center of the building. The front, except for the glass, is constructed of pure white terra cotta and the entrance is in marble and mosaic. The structure will be of the Gothic style of architecture. Freight and passenger elevators will be in the building and each floor will have toilet-rooms. S. S.Berman is the architect.

The Studebaker Building

In addition to their business, the Studebaker Brothers were active in national politics, and for the most part the brothers backed Republican candidates and their policies. The *Rochester Republican* reprinted an account of a meeting in Chicago in August 1884 where Peter Studebaker extolled the economic virtues of protective tariffs: "Mr. Studtbaker said: 'I remember distinctly the good times before the war so often talked about. We then had a comparatively small public debt, and had the revenues from the sales of the small public lands. The tariff was low, but our industries were lower still. We had a tariff for 'revenue exclusively,' and no Republican war debt to pay, yet we paid 63 per yard for calico when it was at its lowest point. Every manufactured article made abroad cost more than it does now under the present 'robber tariff' and the only defense our people had against the high prices was in spinning and weaving the most of their own goods. Farm hands were paid at the highest $13 per month. Corn sold as high as thirty-eight cents. Wheat once reached eighty, but the spurt was only temporary, for it fell back to sixty in a few weeks. Horses sold at from $35 to $60, and the best cows could be purchased at $15 or $20. Hogs sometimes reached $3.75 per hundred, but the average price from 1810 to 1860 was about $2. Butter sold from six to ten cents per pound, and eggs ranged from three to eight cents per dozen, and at points remote from rivers and fast transportation there was no market for farm products except the cereals and live stock. In those days we sold wagons at retail at $110 which we now sell at $80. Plows which then sold for $12 are now sold for $6. Labor of every kind commands from 25 to 60 per cent, more now than it did then, while every manufactured or imported article which labor uses or consumes sells from 20 to 200 per cent, cheaper than it did before the war, and the only articles which command higher prices are those products on the farm.'"

In 1884, Republican James G. Blaine ran for president against Democrat Grover Cleveland, and during the race the Studebaker brothers were accused in national newspapers of coercing their employees to vote for Blaine. A letter to the *Cleveland Commercial Gazette* in December asserted, "The most dastardly attempt that I have seen was practiced, or attempted on the Studebaker Bros. Manufacturing Company at South Bend, Ind., and with considerable success. Just before the election they received threatening letters from different sections, charging them with advertising to their own men that their services would not be required if they did not vote the Republican ticket in November, threatening to withdraw their patronage from such a black Republican firm."

The rumors enraged Democratic voters, especially in the South, where Studebaker wagons were burned by crowds of angry farmers, most notably in Texas. This prompted a response signed by 900 of the company's workers, which was published in the *Saint Joseph Daily Gazette*: "*To the people of Dodd, Sherman, Gainesville, and Honey Grove, Texas and elsewhere in the South and West:* Whereas, It has been brought to our attention that in the towns mentioned in the foregoing, Studebaker wagons have been publicly burned to express popular disapproval of the alleged bulldozing by Studebaker Bros. Mfg. Co. for the coercion of their employees to vote the Republican ticket, it being alleged specially that the Studebaker Bros. Mfg. Co. issued a circular previous to the late election, or caused to be posted on a bulletin in their works, or made other public or private threats that if the said employees did not vote for Blaine and Logan, or other candidates on the Republican ticket, they would be discharged, or experience other mark of the company's disapproval on this account, therefore, *Resolved,* That the undersigned office men, foreman and all other employees of the said Studebaker Brothers manufacturing company, Republicans and Democrats, each speaking for himself, and without fear or favor, declare that these charges, both in letter and in spirit, are utterly and wickedly false, and insult to his manhood and an unmerited and a mischievously designed stigma upon his employers. We have exercised the utmost liberty, when not at actual labor, to talk about whatever political sentiments suited us, to favor whatever political ticket we pleased, and our votes and our speeches at the recent election, and all previous elections, have been free and untrammeled in every respect."

Along with politics, the Studebaker family was deeply involved in various business and philanthropic enterprises in South Bend and throughout Indiana, and one such enterprise concerned the provisioning of the state of Indiana with three new hospitals for the mentally ill. The state government announced in 1883 that one of the new hospitals would be built in Evansville, while the other two would be chosen by a legislative commission charged with visiting possible sites and making the final selections. South Bend, along with numerous other towns and cities in Indiana, entered the fray. Young noted, "The South Bend City Council named a committee to make suitable preparations for the reception of the legislative commission. Among others, committee members included Mayor Ham, Mr. James liver, president of the Oliver Chilled Plow Company, Judge Thomas Stanfield, and Mr. J. M. Studebaker of the Studebaker Brothers Manufacturing Company. The committee met on April 13 of 1883 to discuss possible sites and organized themselves. Mayor Ham took responsibility for presenting the 'sanitary' conditions of South Bend and the surroundings. Judge Stanfield was detailed to discuss the railroads with the visitors, Mr. Oliver (who had built the city's best hotel) was responsible for accommodations and J. M. Studebaker took charge of local transportation and the preparation of statistics. The commission visited South Bend on May 17th of that year...they spent the evening, stayed overnight at the Oliver Hotel and the following day toured the city and several nearby locations in Studebaker carriages. Sites considered included both the Henry Studebaker and the Peter Studebaker farms. The commission's day concluded with a visit to Notre Dame, a concert by the college's Cornet Band and a sumptuous dinner at the hotel. Clem Studebaker spent the day accompanying the commission on its tours." In spite of their efforts, South Bend was not awarded one of the two asylums.

Clement Studebaker's involvement in South Bend went far beyond his role as the company's president. He invested in several other businesses in the city. One, the South Bend Fuel and Gas Company, was the corporate successor to the South Bend Gas Light Company, founded in 1868 by Clement and John M. The company built a coal gas plant at Jefferson and Pearl Streets. Another was the South Bend Malleable Iron company, where Clement served on the Board of Directors. Young also listed some of Clements non-business activities, which included the following:

    South Bend City councilman from 1870-1872

    St. Joseph county councilman from the founding of the county council until 1901

    Member of the board of trustees of the Chautauqua Assembly

    Twice represented Indiana in Republican National Conventions

    United States Commissioner from Indiana to the Paris Exposition of 1878 (where Studebaker wagons won several prizes)

    One of 10 members of the U.S. delegation to the Pan-American Congress held in Washington in 1889-1890

    A member of the South Bend lodge of the Odd Fellows

    An advisor to the architect for the new St. Joseph County courthouse built in 1897 and 1898.

The builder of South Bend's Epworth Hospital, the Milburn Memorial chapel and St. Paul's Methodist Church.

A biography of Clement Studebaker written in 1911 summed up his career: "He was a foe without hate, a friend without treachery, a public officer without vices, a private citizen without wrong, a neighbor without reproach, a Christian without hypocrisy, and a man without guilt. He was Caesar without his ambition, Frederick without his tyranny, Napoleon without his selfishness and Washington without his reward. He was as obedient to authority as a servant, and regal in authority as a king. He was as gentle as a woman in life, pure and modest as a virgin in thought, watchful as a Roman Vestal, and as grand in the every day battles of life as Achilles."

In 1887, tragedy struck the Studebaker brothers when Jacob became ill and died suddenly. Jan Young explained the circumstances: "On December 17, 1887...Jacob Studebaker, the youngest of the brothers and first to pass away, died at the age of forty-three. The previous Wednesday, Jacob and J. M. had left for Chicago, Jacob to attend the annual sleigh opening at the Chicago repository and J. M. on his way to California. Late Friday he complained of feeling unless and by Saturday morning there was no doubt of the seriousness of his illness. Peter, who lived on Millionaires' Row (Prairie Avenue) in Chicago near the Pullmans, the Fields, and the Armours, was with him. Telegrams to Clement in Cincinnati and to J. M. enroute alerted them and Clement actually made it to Chicago before Jacob died. A special train was put on by the Lake Shore & Michigan Southern to carry the remains back to South Bend where they lay in state in Jacob's home....He had been brought into the Baptist church by his wife, the former Harriet Chord, and had made substantial contributions. The funeral, held at Jacob's home the following Wednesday, was attended by family and representatives of both the wagon and carriage plants."

The death of Jacob marked the beginning of the end of the Studebaker company being led by the original founding brothers. An important event in the history of the firm was the marriage of John M.'s daughter Grace to Frederick Samuel Fish. Fish was born on February 8, 1852 in Newark, New Jersey, the son of Reverend Henry Clay Fish and Clarissa Jones Fish. After graduating from the University of Rochester in 1873, he studied law and gained admittance to the New Jersey Bar in 1876. He practiced law in Newark and in New York City from 1876-1890, and in addition to his legal career, he had a budding political career in New Jersey. He served as the city attorney of Newark from 1880-1884, he was a member of the New Jersey General Assembly from 1884-1885, and he was a member of the New Jersey Senate from 1885-1887. However, when he and Grace Studebaker married on June 16, 1887, they moved to South Bend, and by 1891, Fish had been named a director of the Studebaker company as well as a director.

Fish

The 1890s were a decade of transition for the Studebaker brothers, who faced a generational transition and a technological one. The firm arguably had dominated the horse-drawn vehicle industry for the better part of 40 years, but interest was growing in "horseless carriages," vehicles powered by artificial means. Inventors had experimented with a variety of designs and propulsion means since at least the 18th century, beginning with steam before progressing to electric vehicles and a variety of internal combustion engines. The familiar design of a four-wheeled vehicle powered by an internal combustion engine can be traced back to a patent filed by George Selden in 1879, but because of amendments filed by Selden, the patent was not formally granted until 1895.

The patent description stated, "The object of my invention is the production of a safe, simple, and cheap road-locomotive light in weight, easy to control, and possessed of sufficient power to overcome any ordinary inclination. The difficulties heretofore encountered in the application of steam to common roads are the great weight of the boiler, engine, water, and water-tanks, the complicated apparatus necessary to adapt the machine to the roughness of the roads which it must traverse, the necessity of the attendance of a skilled engineer to prevent accidents, and the unsightly appearance of the locomotives built on this plan. I have succeeded in overcoming these difficulties by the construction of a road-locomotive propelled by a liquid-hydrocarbon engine of the compression type, of a design which permits it to be operated in connection with the running-gear, so that the full carrying capacity of the body of the vehicle can be utilized for the transport of persons or goods, and which, by dispensing with skilled attendance and with steam-boilers, water, water-tanks, coal, and coal-bunkers, very largely reduced the weight of the machine in proportion to the power produced and enables me, while employing the most condensed form of fuel, to produce a power road-wagon which differs but little in appearance from and is not materially heavier than the carriages in common use, is capable of being managed by persons of ordinary skill at a minimum of trouble and expense, and which possesses sufficient power to overcome any unusual inclination."

Selden

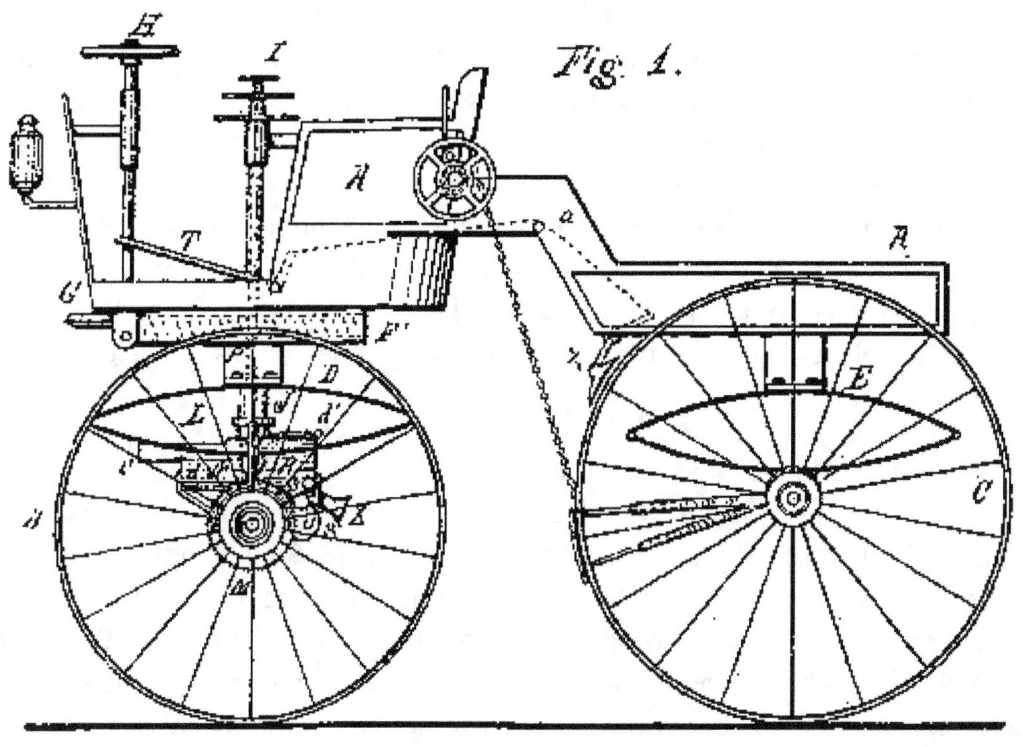

The Selden patent's design

The first practical automobiles along these lines were produced not in America, but in Europe, and before Selden's patent was granted. Karl Benz in Germany in 1888 and Panhard et Levassor in France in 1889 produced automobiles, and in France, Peugeot began production of automobiles in 1892. In the United States, Charles and Frank Duryea formed the Duryea Motor Wagon company in 1893, and after beginning commercial production in 1896, the company sold 13 cars by the end of the year. In 1897, the Autocar Company began operations. By the end of the 1890s, automobile sales were still small, but horseless carriages were clearly the wave of the future.

For the Studebakers, who had built their wealth on the construction and sale of horse-drawn vehicles, the coming of horseless carriages presented a challenge, one each of the brothers faced somewhat differently. Clement and Peter Studebaker vehemently opposed the company moving into automobile production, while John M. was lukewarm. The latter's comparative enthusiasm for the new technology no doubt stemmed from the fact that his son-in-law, Frederick Fish, was enthusiastic about new technology and advocated that the firm evaluate moving into horseless carriages as early as 1895. Little progress was made since Peter was firmly in charge as chairman of the Studebaker Brothers Manufacturing Company's executive committee.

In 1897, the company faced another loss, one that would lead to a fundamental change in the direction of the business. On October 10, 1897, Peter Studebaker died. Jan Young described his death: "Some time in the summer of 1896, Peter had been diagnosed as having heart problems. In those days, of course, the physician could do nothing but counsel a slower schedule and fewer strenuous activities. Peter may or may not have paid much attention to the doctor's advice. Late in September of 1897, Clement, Peter and J.M. Studebaker were invited to be the guests of honor at a reunion in their boyhood home of Ashland, Ohio. Upon their return to South Bend, Peter went horseback riding and had a heart attack. He partially recovered, but a second attack occurred two days later. The day after the second attack, Peter felt able to travel, so he and his brother, J. M. Studebaker, went to Alma, Michigan for treatment in a sanitarium. Three days later, on October 9, Peter woke his brother in the middle of the night, medicine was given, and he went back to sleep. The next day, Peter remained in bed. Shortly before noon, he asked J. M. for a glass of water and then died, at least figuratively in his brother's arms, while drinking the water."

After Peter's death, Fish took his place as chairman of the executive committee in 1897, and from there, he was able to initiate the first steps in pushing the company into the production of motor vehicles. He successfully persuaded the board to earmark $4,000 to the development of a practical electric-powered vehicle. Electricity was decided on first for a couple of reasons. First, they were already making electric carriage bodies for tazies under contract for The New York Electric Vehicle Company. Second, John M. objected to steam and gasoline engines as noisy, dirty, and dangerous, whereas battery power, on the other hand, was considered safer. The experiments and testing resulted in one vehicle being produced.

Rise and Fall

In 1902, the company entered the world of motor vehicle production when the Studebaker Electric Runabout rolled off the assembly line. An early advertisement for Studebaker Automobiles said, "A Motor-Vehicle Worthy of the Studebaker Name. WE have not been indifferent to the introduction of the horseless carriage. Rather than push upon the market and imperfect and immature product, however, we have expended time and money in order to secure a type of automobile which would not discredit our standing in the vehicle world. The Studebaker Electric Vehicle is admirably simple in construction, safe, easy to operate and remarkably free from vibration and noise. It is not a racing machine, but a strongly built practical motor-vehicle for everyday service on country roads and city streets. Extensive experiments and tests have convinced us that the electric motor, with the great improvements recently made in storage batteries, provides the most desirable equipment in every way. It is simplicity itself, clean, odorless, durable and sufficiently speedy for all practical purposes."

NO. 1354. STUDEBAKER RUNABOUT
STICK SEAT. NO TOP

The first vehicles were sold through their wagon showrooms in New York, Chicago, Kansas City, San Francisco, Denver, Salt Lake City, Portland, and Dallas. The first sale actually occurred five days before the company's 50th anniversary to one F.W. Blees of Macon, Missouri. Young wrote of this pioneering automobile owner, "Frederick Wilhelm Victor Blees was born in Aachen, Germany on March 30, 1860, the son of a wealthy iron and coal mine owner. He attended school and entered the Prussian army, but decided that the life of a soldier was not for him and returned to school to study music and the classics. When the government seized his father's mines in retribution for the elder Blees' dissent against its militaristic policies, the younger Blees left for America. After a short stint as a store clerk , Blees met and married the daughter of a wealthy cotton merchant. He then ran a private school in Louisiana and served as an aide-de-camp on the staff of the governor, where he advanced to the rank of colonel. In 1890, Blees accepted the position of superintendent of St. James Academy in Macon, Missouri and moved his family there." Blees' father won a large settlement from the Prussian government in compensation for the seizure of his mines, but he had died in 1895, leaving his entire fortune to his son. Blees invested half a million dollars of his own money in St. James Academy, renaming it Blees Military Academy. How he came to purchase the first Studebaker motor vehicle is unclear.

The fact that the great inventor and innovator Thomas A. Edison purchased the second Studebaker electric vehicle may come as no surprise. What may be more surprising, however, is that it was not his first electric vehicle. Thomas Kinney noted, "The inventor counted Walter Baker among his close friends, and in 1899 he purchased the Baker Motor Vehicle Company's very first product, a sprightly three-quarter horsepower electric buggy. Not surprisingly, the apostle of electricity predicted a tremendous future for electrically propelled vehicles, and his opinion carried weight. So too did the electric itself, whose own power source formed its heaviest component and single greatest drawback, Edison responded with characteristic flair when telling a colleague 'I don't think Nature would be so unkind as to withhold the secret of a good storage battery if a real earnest hunt for it is made. I'm going to hunt.' By the time he became a Studebaker owner, Edison had already embarked on a campaign to improve the led-acid storage battery, a task that would occupy him for several years."

A picture of Edison on his 1903 Studebaker

If the publicity from the sale to Edison helped Studebaker sell other electric vehicles that same year, the bottom line didn't reflect it. The company only sold 18 others in 1902, truly disappointing figures for a company long used to five-figure annual sales.

As the company was transitioning into motor vehicle production, the company lost another brother when Clement passed away in 1901. Young explained, "Clement Studebaker had been in failing health for about a year, diagnosed with pernicious anemia and both heart and digestive problems. On the advice of J. Pierpont Morgan and Andrew Carnegie, he traveled to a spa in southern France and appeared to benefit from it. Upon returning, however, he fell as he was disembarking from the ship in New York and it appears that the fall took back whatever benefits he had received from the trip. Clement lived another six or eight weeks following his return, but during this time his health continued to decline. On Monday November 25, he experienced some delirium, lost consciousness the following day and except for one short period of a few minutes, never regained it. He finally died just before noon on Wednesday, November 27...Clement's funeral was one of the largest and most important to be held in South Bend in decades...The funeral was held at Tippecanoe Place, with Clement's remains on view from 8 to 10 AM for Studebaker employees and from 10 AM to Noon for the general public. The Studebaker employees formed at the north edge of the plant and walked across the railroad tracks to the Studebaker home in file. A New York Central railroad engineer, apparently out of respect for the funeral, actually held his long train at the crossing rather than wait for him to pass."

With Clement's death, the last substantive opposition to Studebaker's entry into motor vehicle production eroded, though John M. still looked to horse-drawn wagons as the basis for the company's fortunes. To some extent, he was correct, because while the company sold less than two dozen electric vehicles in 1902, wagon sales topped $4,000,000 that same year. Under Fred Fish's direction, however, Studebaker continued to work on their electric vehicles, making refinements, pursuing foreign sales, and adding new types, including a truck and light delivery wagon.

The primary market for electric vehicle sales were to women, and the company recognized that by introducing elegantly styled vehicles like the Victoria. A 1905 advertisement told readers, "The handsome 1905 Victoria Phaeton presented herewith is indisputably the most satisfactory electric automobile yet produced. It is especially designed for city and suburban driving. The mechanism for its operation and control is the simplest and surest ever put into an electric car." While still selling an electric vehicle, that same advertisement promoted a gasoline powered automobile: "The 1905 Studebaker Gasoline Automobile for distance touring possesses many admirable features. Most notable are its ease of starting (by one turn of the crank), made sure control by foot lever, absence of vibration and the accessibility of all working parts."

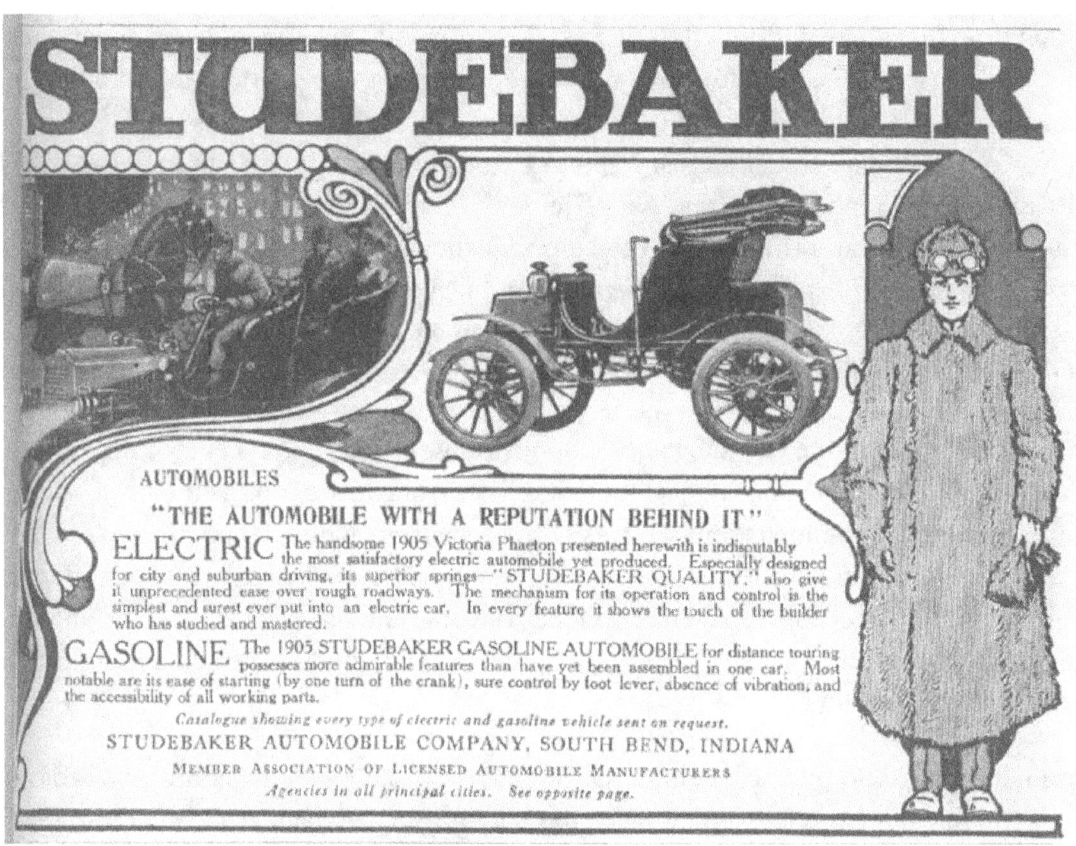

The 1905 Electric Studebaker

The advertisement reveals much about Studebaker's strategy in entering the motor vehicle market under Fish. In the early years of the automotive industry, no one could predict which propulsion system would be standard. Would vehicles be powered by clean but relatively inefficient batteries, or would they rely on the dirtier and more dangerous but more efficient gasoline powered engines? Most firms had to settle on one or the other, but Studebaker was a well-established company with resources start-up automakers did not have. Under Fish's direction, the company pursued gasoline-powered vehicles as they continued to produce electric cars.

Lacking the precision metalworkers necessary to build cars from the ground up, Fish entered into negotiations in 1904 with the Garford Manufacturing Company, an established builder of automobile chassis. The agreement was that Studebaker would buy into Garford, with Garford providing the frame, drive train, and engines to Studebaker, which would provide the bodies. As part of this, Fish organized the Studebaker Automobile Company that same year as a separate entity from Studebaker Brothers. The first Studebaker-Garford rolled out of the factory on July 22, 1904. It was purchased by H. D. Johnson, John M. Studebaker;s son-in-law, for $2,000. This marked the real beginning of Studebaker's involvement in the automobile industry. For 1904, the Studebaker produced about 100,000 vehicles, though most of them were still pulled by horses.

The Studebaker-Garfords were popular cars. Sales grew, with combined sales figures for wagons and automobiles topping out at $7,800,000 in 1907. Most of this increase was directly attributed to automobile sales, but demand for new vehicles was beginning to outpace Studebaker's ability to supply them. Garford could not supply the components fast enough because a new factory they had under construction was affected by delays and labor problems. Studebaker eventually acquired Garford through a stock purchase, but that was still not enough for the company to meet its growing demand.

A 1908 Studebaker-Garford B limousine

In order to remedy the demand problem, Fish entered into an agreement, approved by John Studebaker, with the new E-M-F Company in 1908. E-M-F Company was a small conglomerate of seven companies put together by merger and acquisition to build medium-priced automobiles in large numbers. The organizers of the company were Barney Everitt, William Metzger, and Walter Flanders. While they had the factories and equipment, E-M-F had no way to market their cars, so under the agreement, E-M-F would manufacture the cars and Studebaker would sell them through their existing national sales network. They were marketed as medium-priced models, the '20 and '30, selling for $1,000 and $1,250. In the following 16 months Studebaker sold over 8,000 cars, By the end of 1910, sales stood at over 15,000.

While the arrangement was proving profitable, there were serious problems. Most notably, E-M-Fs cars were proving to be very unreliable; for example, the '20 had faulty transmissions and clutches. The company's reluctance to fixing the engineering issues angered John M. Compounding this, there was infighting among the three executives in E-M-F, and eventually, Everitt and Metzger left the company in the middle of 1909. After that, Fish arranged for Studebaker to buy-out E-M-F. Thus, on December 31, 1910, E-M-F and Studebaker Brothers Manufacturing Company were merged to form The Studebaker Corporation, a new entity incorporated in New Jersey on February 14, 1911. The new company was organized as before, with John M. Studebaker as President and Chairman of the Board and Fred Fish as First Vice President.

One of the first things the new company did was halt all production of existing vehicles to correct the design flaws. Fish sent mechanics to the owners of every '20 and had the bad transmissions and other faulty parts replaced at a cost to the company of over $1,000,000.

By the time Studebaker restarted production in 1911, there were a couple of significant changes. Electric vehicles were dropped completely, an acknowledgement that for the foreseeable future the automobile industry would be dominated by the internal combustion engine. The cars all carried the Studebaker marque, an acknowledgment that the company was fully committed to the automobile manufacturing business. Prices on new cars were cut and each included a generous warranty. By the end of 1911, the new company had sold 22,555 cars, grossing $28,480,000.

The next several years saw the continued expansion of the Studebaker Company, and along with the expansion came a change in the leadership. In 1913, John M. celebrated his 80th birthday, an event that was commemorated in memorable fashion. The *South Bend Tribune* reported, "With one accord the men and women who had worked for years to help make the name of Studebaker famous made ready to honor the man who had been at the head of the industry for nearly two generations. All the employees formed in a line to shake hands with Mr. Studebaker, who took his stand near the entrance to the administration building. He gathered around him as a kind of reception committee seven men who had been with the company over 40 years. When the handshaking was over the employees were served with refreshments which Mr. Studebaker had provided for them."

In 1915, John M. stepped aside from the daily operations of the company, assuming the title of Honorary President. That July, Albert Erskine became President and Fish became Chairman of the Board of Directors. John M. Studebaker, the last of the company's original founders, died on March 16, 1917 after suffering from leukemia for the previous six years. Like the others, Young described his funeral: "[John Mohler Studebaker's] funeral was held at his home, Sunnyside. The Studebaker Corporation was closed for the day, Businesses throughout the city closed late in the afternoon and the streetcar system came to a halt for five minutes. Carnations were J. M.'s favorite flower and a basket of them was provided for the mourners to place on the bier as a tribute. At. J. M.'s direction, the viewing was open to all, regardless of their social position and hundreds from the factory came, many with 20 or 30 or more years of service."

With John Mohler's death, an era had come to a close for the company, and somewhat fittingly, the era of the horse-drawn wagon was also closing rapidly. When Albert Erskine wrote his history of the firm in 1918, he recorded that the seven Studebaker plants had an annual capacity of 100,000 automobiles, 75,000 horse-drawn vehicles, and $10,000,000 of automotive spare parts and harnesses. The trend was unmistakable, and in 1919, Erskine ordered the removal of the last wagon gear. With that, the Studebaker Corporation's last connection to the original company formed by the Studebaker brothers in the 1850s was severed.

The company continued for several more decades without a Studebaker at its head. It was a profitable company through the 1920s, with the number of models expanding to 50 by 1929. As with most companies, however, it found itself unprepared for the Wall Street crash in October 1929, and suddenly the company was unable to sell even lower-priced automobiles. Due to a series of bad financial decisions, the company entered receivership in March 1933. It emerged, however, in December 1933, and the entire organization was refinanced and reorganized on March 9, 1935. The company remained profitable through the lean years of the late 1930s, and like much of the rest of the country, its fortunes only revived fully after America joined World War II. With domestic automotive production halted, Studebaker turned to military vehicle manufacturing, turning out the Studebaker US6 truck and the M29 Weasel cargo and personnel carrier.

A Studebaker US6 truck

The M29 Weasel

Although Studebaker began churning out products in World War II and its aftermath, the 1950s brought the beginning of the end for Studebaker. The company's cautious management team failed to meet the challenges posed by Ford and General Motors. When Ford discounted its cars after a massive increase in production in 1953 as part of an attempt to regain the title of the largest car maker in the world, Studebaker found itself unable to compete. This combined with ballooning labor costs and quality control issues caused the company severe financial problems, and by 1954 the company was losing money. A merger with Packard failed to stem the tide, and by 1956 the company was nearly bankrupt.

There was a temporary revival of fortunes in the late 1950s and early 1960s when Studebaker began to manufacture the compact Lark, but by 1962, sales fell steadily as rumors circulated that Studebaker was leaving the automotive business. The company struggled on, but on December 20, 1963, the last Studebaker automobile rolled off the assembly line in South Bend.

The 1960 Studebaker Lark

Today, the name Studebaker is kept alive through organizations of car enthusiasts and Internet websites dedicated to documenting the history of the company and its cars. Perhaps the most famous is the most unusual. In the 1920s, the Studebaker company set up a car proving ground to test its vehicles. In 1938, a grove of 8,000 pine trees was planted in a pattern that, viewed from above, spells out Studebaker. The tree sign was placed on the National Register of Historic Places in 1985, and in 1987 the Guinness Book of World Records listed it as the world's "largest living advertisement sign." In 2004, the sign was severely damaged by an ice storm, but between 2012 and 2015, dead and diseased trees were removed and replaced with 2,000 pine saplings, ensuring that the location – and the various classic Studebaker cars still being restored and preserved – will keep the Studebaker name alive.

Online Resources

Other 19th century history titles by Charles River Editors

Other 20th century history titles by Charles River Editors

Other books about Studebaker on Amazon

Further Reading

Erskine, A R History of the Studebaker Corporation, South Bend (1918)

Longstreet, Stephen A Century on Wheels: The Story of Studebaker, A History, 1852–1952, Henry Holt and Co, N.Y. (1952)

Bonsall, Thomas E More Than They Promised: The Studebaker Story Stanford University Press (2000)

Foster, Patrick Studebaker: America's Most Successful Independent Automaker Motorbooks

Severson A. Lark and Super Lark: The Last Days of Studebaker. Ate Up With Motor, October 17, 2009

Free Books by Charles River Editors

We have brand new titles available for free most days of the week. To see which of our titles are currently free, click on this link.

Discounted Books by Charles River Editors

We have titles at a discount price of just 99 cents everyday. To see which of our titles are currently 99 cents, click on this link.